D0904661

Springs of Hope

Goethe
Seneca
Shakespeare
Shelley
Tagore

Marcel Schurman Company Inc.
Oakland CA 94608

At the edge of despair dawns a clarity in which one is almost happy.

JEAN ANOUILH

Hope is the thing
   with feathers
That perches in
   the soul
And sings the tune
without the words,
And never stops
   at all
And sweetest in the
   gale is heard.

EMILY DICKINSON

Misfortune is an occasion to
demonstrate character.

SENECA

What is man finally left with? Hope.

DIOGENES

There is a
law in life:
when one
door closes
to us
another
one opens.

ANDRÉ GIDE

WE DO NOT
BECOME FREE
BY REFUSING
TO ACKNOW-
LEDGE SOME-
THING ABOVE
US, BUT BY
RESPECTING
SOMETHING
ABOVE US.

GOETHE

As long as hope remains, only the coward will despair. BERTRAND RUSSELL.

Hopeless-ness is anticipated defeat.

KARL JASPERS

Deprive the
average man of
his life's illusions,
and you rob
him of his
happiness.

IBSEN

Should a single disappointed hope make us so hostile towards the world?

LESSING

Hope walks with life,
only in death does hope end. THEOCRITUS

Hope is like the clouds: some pass by, others bring rain.

ABU AL ALA AL MAARRI

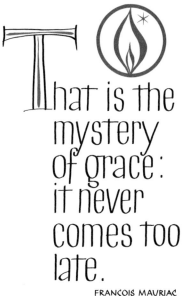

That is the
mystery
of grace:
it never
comes too
late.

FRANÇOIS MAURIAC

Love your
calling with
passion,
it is the
meaning
of your
life. AUGUSTE RODIN

O Wind,
If Winter comes, can Spring be far behind?

SHELLEY

True hope is swift,
and flies with
swallow's wings;

Kings it makes gods,
and meaner
creatures kings.

SHAKESPEARE

I slept and dreamed
that life was joy,

I awoke and saw
that life was duty,

I acted, and behold:
duty was joy.

TAGORE

If you have hoped and your expectation was not fulfilled, then go on hoping.

TALMUD

We have no ultimate assurance,
we have only hope.

ERNST BLOCH

The most
distant goal
is attainable
to him who
hopes wisely.

LOPE DE VEGA

The boldest and
most ridiculous
hope has sometimes
been the cause of
extraordinary
        success.

VAUVENARGUES
t

Precious little gifts of lasting value.

In the same series:

SPRINGS OF COMFORT
SPRINGS OF FRIENDSHIP
SPRINGS OF HAPPINESS
SPRINGS OF INDIAN WISDOM
SPRINGS OF JAPANESE WISDOM
SPRINGS OF JEWISH WISDOM
SPRINGS OF MUSIC
SPRINGS OF ORIENTAL WISDOM
SPRINGS OF PERSIAN WISDOM
SPRINGS OF HOPE
SPRINGS OF LOVE
SPRINGS OF JOY

Texts chosen by E. Hettinger / Translated by Dr. Peter M. Daly
Designer: J. Tannheimer, Modèle déposé, BIRPI
Acknowledgements: Illustrations: Roses
by Lotte Günthart, Regensberg-Zürich

Marcel Schurman Company Inc.

Oakland CA 94608

Printed in Switzerland